SCHIRMER'S LIBR.
OF MUSICAL CLASSICS

Vol. 811

MUZIO CLEMENTI

Op. 36

Six Sonatinas

For the Piano

Revised and Fingered by

LOUIS KÖHLER

Second Piano Parts Published Separately

ISBN 978-0-7935-2569-0

G. SCHIRMER, Inc.

DISTRIBUTED BY

HAL•LEONARD®
CORPORATION
7777 W. BLUEMOUND RD. P.O. BOX 13819 MILWAUKEE, WI 53213

SONATINA.

Op. 36, Nº 1.

Spiritoso.

M. CLEMENTI.

SONATINA.

Op. 36, Nº 2.

Muzio Clementi

Allegretto.

2.

Allegretto

8

Allegro.

SONATINA.
Op. 36, Nº 3.

Spiritoso.

3.

Un poco adagio

Allegro

SONATINA.

Op. 36, No. 4.

Con spirito.

4.

Andante con espressione.

Rondo
Allegro vivace

Da Capo al Fine.

SONATINA.
Op. 36, Nº 5.

Muzio Clementi

Air Suisse (Original.)

Allegro moderato.

Rondo
Allegro di molto

SONATINA.
Op. 36, No 6.

Allegro con spirito.

MUZIO CLEMENTI

Rondo.
Allegretto spiritoso